Contents

Acknowledgements
Text by Peter Hirst. The publishers
would like to thank John Jaques (page 4)
for their photographic contribution to
this book. Photographs on front and
back cover courtesy of Empics. All oth[er]
photographs courtesy of the
International Table Tennis Federation
(ITTF) and U at the Game.

Illustrations by Dave Saunders (pages 13,
14, and 18) and Ron Dixon at TechType.

1

Foreword

Administration

Table tennis is one of the world's largest indoor participation sports. It is a full Olympic sport, and it can be played as a highly athletic and exciting competitive activity or as a relaxing and healthy recreation. It is truly a sport for all. Table tennis can be played by the young and old, by males and females, by the fit and not so fit, by the able-bodied and those with disabilities. In fact, anyone can play and enjoy this great game.

Note Throughout the book players are referred to individually as 'he'. This should, of course, be taken to mean 'he or she' where appropriate.

The International Table Tennis Federation (ITTF), made up of member countries' national governing body associations, is responsible for the game's rules.

The European Table Tennis Union (ETTU) is responsible for competitive play in Europe.

The English Table Tennis Association Ltd (ETTA) is the governing body of the sport in England.

The English Schools Table Tennis Association (ESTTA) is an organisation backed by the ETTA, and is responsible for all school competitions.

The British Table Tennis Association for People with Disabilities (BTTAD) is another organisation backed by the ETTA, and is responsible for all training and competitions that are specifically organised for disabled players.

Further details of all these associations can be obtained from:

The General Secretary
English Table Tennis Association Ltd
Queensbury House
Havelock Road
Hastings
East Sussex
TN34 1HF

tel: 01424 722525
fax: 01424 422103
email: admin@ettahq.freeserve.co.uk
website: www.etta.co.uk

Equipment

The table

Table tennis tables are 2.74 m x 1.525 m (9 ft x 5 ft), with a surface thickness of 22–25 mm (0.8–0.98 in).

The table stands 76 cm (2 ft 6 in) above the floor. Smaller mini-tables are available. Tables are:

- standard – with two separate halves
- rollaway – the two halves are mounted on a central wheeled under-carriage for easy manoeuvrability
- rollaway with playback – a rollaway where one half may be vertical while the other half is horizontal. This allows for one player to practise alone.

Tables are the most expensive item of equipment and should be well cared for. Tables should be stored 'face to face' to prevent the surface from being scratched. They should be stored on the central edge since damage to this edge will not affect play.

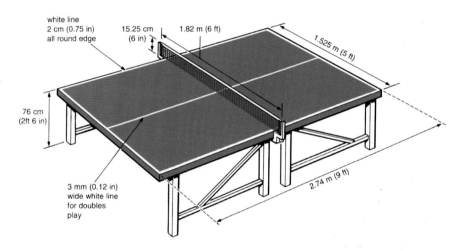

white line 2 cm (0.75 in) all round edge

15.25 cm (6 in)

1.82 m (6 ft)

1.525 m (5 ft)

76 cm (2ft 6 in)

3 mm (0.12 in) wide white line for doubles play

2.74 m (9 ft)

▲ *Fig. 1 The table's dimensions and markings*

The net and posts

The top of the net is 15.25 cm (6 in) above the playing surface. The net posts clamp to the playing top so that the net is held firmly in place. The net usually has a cord through the top of it so that the tension can be adjusted. Most nets and posts can be removed from the table for easy storage.

The ball

Balls are made of celluloid or plastic, and are white or orange in colour. The ball is 40 mm (1.57 in) in diameter and weighs 2.7 g (0.09 oz). The quality of the ball is determined by a 'star' rating: the higher the rating, the higher the quality. All official competitions are played with three-star celluloid balls.

The bat

Table tennis bats (or 'rackets') may be of any size, shape or weight. They are made of a wooden blade and normally two rubbers. (Penhold players – *see* page 8 – may use a bat with rubber on only one side of the blade.)

The blades are made from several layers (or ply) of wood. The number of ply and the softness or hardness of the wood affects the speed and control of the blade. Greater speed generally means less control. Slow blades are made of three-ply soft wood, whereas very fast blades may be seven-ply with additional layers of carbon fibre.

The rubbers have a smooth side and a pimpled side. Most are used in conjunction with a layer of sponge which may be of varying thicknesses – 1.0–2.5 mm (0.04–0.1 in). The total thickness of the covering (rubber and sponge) on either side must not be more than 4 mm (0.16 in).

Rubbers are usually reversed pimples (smooth side out) but some players use combination bats, i.e. different rubbers on each side of the blade.

Rubbers must be red on one side of the blade and black on the other side. In the case of a penhold player where only one sheet of rubber is used, the bat must still be red on one side and black on the other. This is usually achieved by staining the blade.

The beginner should choose a five-ply all-round bat with 1.5 mm (0.06 in) rubbers. This will give good control and reasonable spin.

Clothing

Table tennis is a fast, athletic game and clothing should be comfortable and should not restrict movement. Short-sleeved shirts and shorts are normally worn. Clothing should be sweat-absorbent and of a colour that is not the same as the ball. Socks may be of any colour but are usually white. Playing shoes should have a good grip but must be light and flexible for the fast movements that are required. The shoes should support the heel and instep.

Lighting

Local conditions will vary considerably, but good even lighting is a priority in table tennis. Tungsten halogen lights give the best lighting. Ideally, lights should be about 4 m (13 ft) from the floor.

Spin

Table tennis is often said to be a game of touch. This is true, but it is also a game of spin.

The ball is generally struck with either 'topspin' or 'backspin'. In addition, 'sidespin' may be added. If there is little or no spin on the ball, it is referred to as 'float'.

Topspin

Topspin is produced by starting the stroke below and/or behind the ball and contacting the ball as lightly as possible, i.e. brushing the ball in an upward and forward motion.

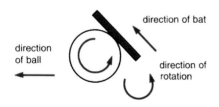

▲ *Fig. 2 Topspin*

Backspin

Backspin is produced by starting the stroke above and/or behind the ball and contacting the ball as lightly as possible, i.e. brushing the ball in a downward and/or forward motion.

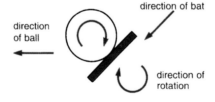

▲ *Fig. 3 Backspin*

Sidespin

Sidespin is produced by brushing across the ball lightly. This spin can be imparted in addition to topspin or backspin.

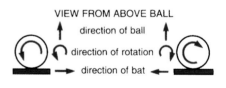

▲ *Fig. 4 Sidespin*

The effect of spin

The use of excessive spin is particularly effective on the serve.

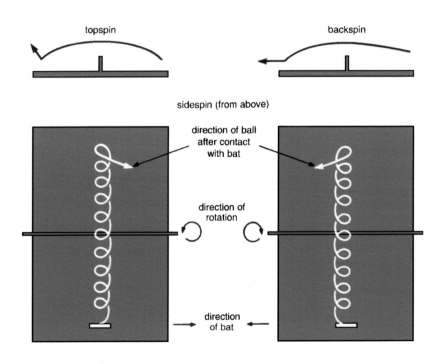

topspin

backspin

sidespin (from above)

direction of ball
after contact
with bat

direction of
rotation

direction
of bat

The grip

The grip controls the angle of the bat, which in turn influences the ball in many ways:

- height
- depth
- speed
- type of spin
- amount of spin
- degree of touch.

The 'shake hands' style is where the thumb and forefinger lay on the blade of the bat, with the three remaining fingers loosely around the handle in the palm of the hand.

The 'penhold' grip is popular in Asian countries, but has restrictions since generally only one side of the bat is used.

It is advisable to adopt one of the grips suggested above for all open play.

Coaching tip

Keep the three fingers on the handle of the bat as loose as possible to decrease muscle tension in the forearm and retain the maximum degree of touch.

▲ ▼ *'Shake hands' grip*

▼ *'Penhold' grip*

Bat angles

Table tennis is an 'open skill' sport. This means that the environment is forever changing and that players need to adapt on a constant basis, as every approaching ball will be different in some way.

As each ball will have a different spin, speed, direction and trajectory, then one of the prime skills of a player is perception, in order to adjust the:

- angle of bat
- angle of swing
- degree of touch

to adapt to each situation.

When striking the ball, the bat angle is referred to as 'open' where the bat is sloping backwards, or 'closed' where the bat is sloping forwards.

An open angle will neutralise an approaching ball which has 'backspin', and a fast-moving swing in an upward direction with a closed angle will increase the spin on the ball with

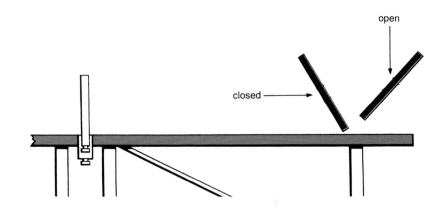

▲ *Fig. 6 Bat angles*

the ball still rotating on the same axis.

A closed angle of bat will neutralise an approaching ball with 'topspin', and an open angle moving fast in a downward direction will increase the spin on the ball with the ball still rotating on the same axis.

Coaching tip
Watch your opponent's bat action very closely as this will give you the invaluable information required for a successful stroke execution.

10

Striking point

The striking point is the position where the ball is ideally struck in relation to the upper part of the body. Where possible, contact the ball at about chest height and equal distance from each shoulder. This is often referred to as the 'natural height and distance of point of contact'. It is of advantage if this can remain the same each time the ball is struck and for all strokes, as it will enhance stroke production and rhythm.

Use the free hand as a 'radar' system by pointing and tracing the ball. Strike when the ball is adjacent to the free hand.

Coaching tip
Adopting the same striking position aids overall ball control and accuracy.

Developing stroke play, ball control and bat angle skills

Perception

● Ready position – the position in which a player should both start and finish each time they strike the ball. The position is determined solely by the target that is selected (*see* figs 7, 8 and 9).
● Read the play – watch your opponent's body language, their speed and direction of swing, the angle of bat and then the ball.
● Radar – use the free hand as a radar system, tracking the ball during the rally.

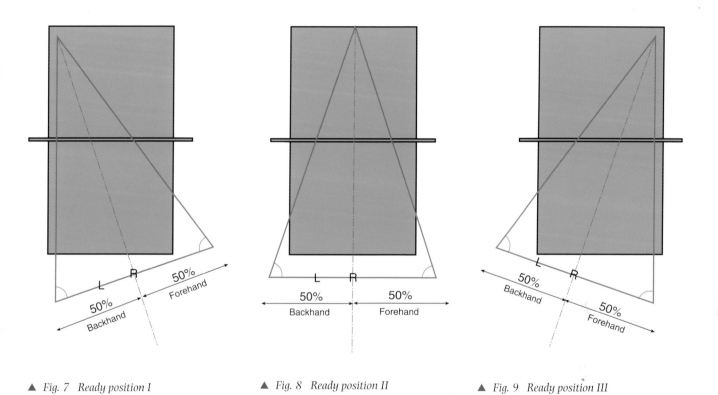

▲ *Fig. 7 Ready position I*

▲ *Fig. 8 Ready position II*

▲ *Fig. 9 Ready position III*

Decisions

- Timing – try to hit the ball at a high point, as this will allow you to play the ball downwards in a straight line to the target (*see* fig. 10).
- Table position – try to hit the ball as early as possible to find the widest angles with the greatest degree of accuracy (*see* fig. 11).
- Base movement – move from the ready position using the nearest foot to the ball to a position slightly behind the contact point between bat and ball.

Fig. 11 Table positions A, B & C ▶

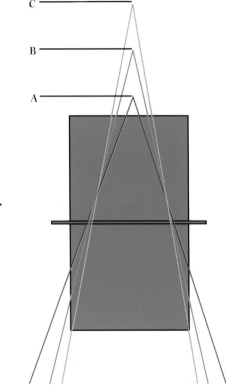

▼ *Fig. 10 Timing point*

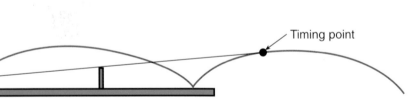

Timing point

Action

• Body action – try to keep the centre of gravity of the body low and at a constant height, leaning from one foot to the other for weight transfer.
• Bat arm – use the shoulder joint for power strokes, the elbow for maximum control and the wrist for speed/spin strokes.
• Ensure that 50% of the forward movement of the bat is before contact with the ball to ensure bat speed.

Coaching tips

• You must watch and read your opponent's actions with great care, adapt to what you see, make good decisions as to where you wish to play the ball from, and act accordingly.
• Link your bat action to where the ball has travelled. This will restrict what your opponent can do in reply and make it easier to read for your next stroke.

Tactical stroke play

Backhand and forehand pushing

Keep the ball low, slow and with two bounces on the receiver's side. The second bounce should be as near to your opponent's baseline as possible. This will inhibit your opponent from attacking with strength, and increase your opportunity to attack with your next stroke. Backhand push strokes are very effective when you are unable to attack the ball.

Perception

- Adopt a ready position in relation to your last target and facing the ball.
- Watch your opponent's actions carefully and track the ball with the free hand.

Decisions

- Try to strike the ball at a high spot, as near to the table as comfortable and moving the nearest foot to the ball.

Action

- Staying in a low posture, strike using an elbow action with 50% of the forward movement of the bat before contact.

▼ *Fig. 12   Pushing: two bounces on the receiver's side; second bounce on the baseline*

Coaching tips

- Keep the three fingers on the bat handle loose.
- With forehand strokes, the upper body should turn back slightly to allow it to return to a facing position on production.

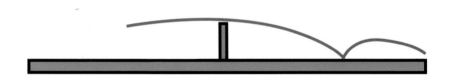

Forehand and backhand topspin driving

Strike the ball early with speed and topspin to a target that is deep and/or angled. This will reduce your opponent's organisation time and potentially increase your own time if your opponent drops back. Use this stroke when the approaching ball has height and/or depth.

Perception

- Adopt a ready position in relation to your last target and facing the ball.
- Watch your opponent's actions carefully and track the ball with the free hand.

Decisions

- Try to strike the ball at a high spot, as near to the table as comfortable, having moved the nearest foot towards the ball.

Action

- Staying in a low posture, strike using a slight but fast rotation of the upper body on forehand strokes, with a shoulder action, with 50% of the forward movement of the bat before contact.

Coaching tips

- Always strike the ball as early as possible for maximum effect.
- With backhand topspin drives, the upper body does not need rotating but stays facing the line of the ball.

Advanced strokes

The block – forehand or backhand

A very short stroke, generally without spin, taken very early and deep and/or angled. It is used to reduce the organisation time of the opponent and/or to neutralise the spin on the ball. You are in a situation where you do not have time to generate speed or spin and would still choose to keep your opponent under pressure.

Perception

- Adopt a ready position in relation to your last target and facing the ball.
- Watch your opponent's actions carefully and track the ball with the free hand.

Decisions

- Try to strike the ball as early as possible and as near to the table as comfortable, having moved the nearest foot towards the ball.

Action

- Staying in a low, crouched position, use as little approach to the ball as possible while striking with a loose wrist action.

Coaching tip

- Strike the ball as early as possible with the fingers on the handle of the bat as loose as possible and with a relaxed wrist.

Forehand and backhand loop

(A variation of forehand topspin driving.)

Strike the ball with as much topspin to a target that is deep and/or angled. This will reduce your opponent's ability to control the ball and will potentially increase your chances of a high return. Use this stroke when the approaching ball is only just high or long enough to attack, or when the approaching ball has excessive backspin.

Perception

• Adopt a ready position in relation to your last target and facing the ball.
• Watch your opponent's actions carefully and track the ball with the free hand.

Decisions

• Try to strike the ball at a high spot, as near to the table as comfortable, having moved the nearest foot towards the ball.

Action

• Staying in a low posture, strike using a slight but fast rotation of the upper body with a shoulder, elbow action with 50% of the forward movement of the bat before contact.

Coaching tip

• Create as much bat speed as possible, but with only a light degree of touch brushing against the ball. This often means that the ball will travel slowly but have extreme spin.
• Keep your grip very loose.

Forehand and backhand chop

Strike the ball early with speed and topspin to a target that is deep and/or angled. This will reduce your opponent's organisation time and potentially increase your own time if your opponent drops back. Use this stroke when the approaching ball has height and/or depth.

Perception

- Adopt a ready position in relation to your last target and facing the ball.
- Watch your opponent's actions carefully and track the ball with the free hand.

Decisions

- Try to strike the ball at a high spot, as near to the table as comfortable, having moved the nearest foot towards the ball.

Action

- Staying in a low posture, strike using a slight but fast rotation of the upper body on forehand strokes, with a shoulder action, with 50% of the forward movement of the bat before contact.

Coaching tips

- Always strike the ball as early as possible for maximum effect.
- With backhand topspin drives, the upper body does not need rotating but stays facing the line of the ball.

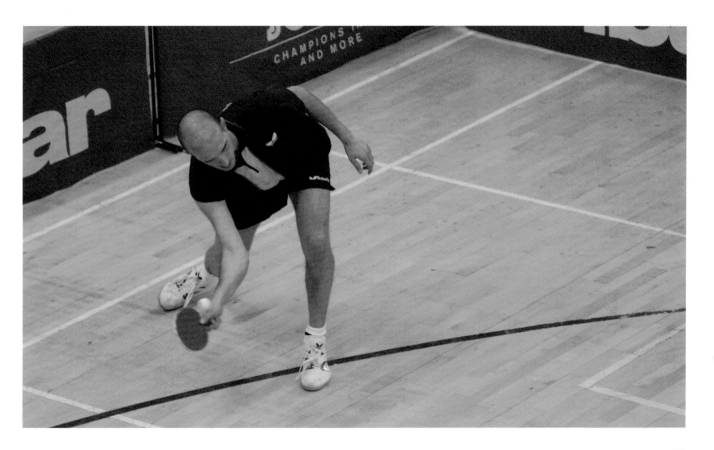

Service

Very good players will use a wide range of services, trying to disguise as much as possible the type of spin, the amount of spin, and the speed and direction of the ball.

Often the advanced player will use forehand services from the backhand side of the table to utilise different angles of play and increase the opportunity to follow up with a very strong forehand topspin loop. The player must be swift of foot for this to be profitable, as the whole table has to be covered with the forehand.

Coaching tip
Use a very loose grip to allow the maximum speed and range of wrist movement.

To serve, the ball must be thrown upwards, without spin, from the open palm of the server's hand so that it rises at least 16 cm. When it is falling from the highest point of its trajectory, it must be struck so that it bounces on the server's half of the table (known as the 'server's court'), passes over or around the net, and then bounces on the receiver's court. For doubles, each court is divided into halves by a white centre line and the ball has to bounce diagonally from the right-hand half of the server's court to the right-hand half of the receiver's court. The centre line is regarded as part of each right-hand half-court, so the service is good if the ball bounces on it.

From the start of service until it is struck, the ball must be behind the server's end line and above the level of the playing surface, and it must not be hidden from the receiver by any part of the body or clothing of the server or of the server's doubles partner.

If in service the ball touches the net but the service is otherwise correct, the umpire calls a 'let'; no point is scored and the service is taken again. The ball is in play from the time at which it leaves the server's hand, so that once it has been thrown a miss or a poor throw will mean that the opponent scores a point. However, if the ball is accidentally dropped before it is thrown, no point is scored because the ball was not in play.

The first server in a match is decided by the toss of a coin. The winner of the toss can choose to serve or receive first, or to start play at a particular end of the table; if the winner decides to serve or receive, the loser can choose an end, and vice versa. The players change ends after every game, and again in the deciding game, when first one player or pair scores 5 points.

Service return

The player receiving the service should be in a ready position, so that he can move easily in any direction to cover every possible angle that the server may use. The stroke used to return service depends on the type of serve, but generally, forehand and backhand topspin drives are used to return top-spin and long serves, while forehand and backhand pushes are used for short serves with backspin. After the ball has been correctly served, play continues until one player fails to make a good return and so loses the point.

A good return is when the ball bounces once only on the receiver's half of the table. It must then be hit (a 'hit' includes the hand holding the bat) and returned to the opponent's side without touching any obstacle (other than the net). There is no height limit to the path of the ball. It may pass above the lights but it must not touch them. If the ball touches any obstacle the ball is 'dead' and the last striker loses the point.

A good return can pass over the net at any point in its length, or around the side of the net post. It is also a good return if the ball passes under the net post.

A player is allowed to follow a spinning ball back across the net and strike it over the opponent's half of the table as long as he does not touch the net or net posts with his bat or clothing.

Warm-up

Cool-down

Before taking part in any physical activity, players should spend at least a few minutes warming up. Warming up helps to warm the muscles and so prevent injury; it also mobilises the joints and raises the heart rate. In short, warm-ups help a player to perform to his best.

The warm-up should start with general body exercises such as light jogging or skipping which should be slowly increased in intensity. These should be followed by static stretching exercises covering the whole body, beginning at the top and working down as follows:

- neck and shoulders (do not roll the neck in a full circle as this may cause damage to the vertebrae)
- arms and chest
- lower back and stomach
- groin and hips
- upper legs
- knees
- lower legs and ankles.

Ballistic stretching exercises, which involve bouncing or jerking movements, could cause injury and so should be avoided.

The warm-up should take place just prior to the beginning of the practice session or match.

Cool-downs after exercise will help to avoid any stiffness or soreness in the muscles. Slow jogging or walking and light stretching are ideal and should be continued for a few minutes until the body returns to a near resting state.

Scoring

In table tennis the scoring system is very simple. Either player or pair may score a point, regardless of which player serves. A point is scored if an opponent:

- fails to make a good service or return
- intercepts the ball before it has bounced when it is above or moving towards the playing surface
- hits the ball twice or lets it bounce twice before hitting it
- moves the table or touches it with his free hand
- touches the net
- in doubles, hits the ball out of turn.

Except in service, it makes no difference whether the ball touches the net while passing over or around it.

A game is won by the first player or pair to score 11 points, unless both have scored 10 points, when the winner is the first player or pair to subsequently gain a lead of 2 points,

eg 15–13. Each player or pair serves for 2 points in turn unless the score reaches 10–10, after which they serve alternately. A match can be the best of any odd number of games, but it is usually 5 or 7.

In doubles, the players must hit the ball alternately and in a strict rotation, so that in each game a player always hits the ball to the same opposing player and receives from the player's partner. There are only 2 possible orders of play: A, X, B, Y, A; or A, Y, B, X, A. If A serves to X in the first game, in the second game either X must serve to A or Y must serve to B. In the third game, A must serve to X or B to Y, and so on. In the deciding game, the order is reversed as soon as either pair scores 5 points.

In each game, the pair with the right to serve first can choose which of them will do so. In the first game the receiving pair can then choose which of them will receive first and in which subsequent game the sequence must be reversed.

The expedite system

The expedite system is the method provided to prevent unduly long games. It is introduced after 10 minutes of play (or at any time earlier if both players or pairs agree). Once the system has been introduced, it remains in force for the remainder of the match.

Under this system, the players serve only one service each in turn and the server has 12 strokes after his service to win the point. If his service and the 12 subsequent strokes are safely returned by the receiver, then the receiver wins the point. The game is won in the normal way by a player winning 11 points, or after 10-all by two clear points.

The expedite system was introduced, like the tie-break in tennis, to encourage the server to attack and so maintain exciting play.

Practice

People play table tennis for different reasons – to socialise, for exercise, for competition or just for fun. Undoubtedly, winning is more enjoyable than losing. To be successful at table tennis, as in every other sport, the player must commit time to practice.

Practice can be divided into two elements:

- practice to improve the strokes, i.e. technical practice
- practice to improve the tactics, i.e. tactical practice.

Technical practice

There are two types of technical practice:

- showing
- testing.

Showing practice is where both players know the direction(s) of the ball, with a specific spin(s) and speed(s) (*see* fig. 13).

This form of practice is very good for technical development and shows players how to recognise the opponent's bat actions and adapt their own actions accordingly.

▼ *Fig. 13 Technical practice: showing (Alt.) = alternate targets*

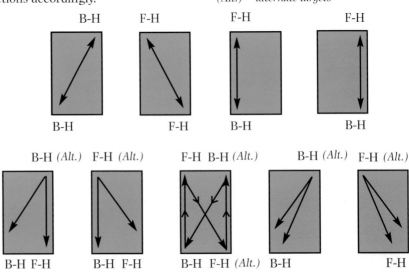

Testing practice is where the player does not know where the ball is going and must rely on their ability to read the opponent's bat angle, direction and speed and react accordingly (*see* fig. 14).

Coaching tip
Both showing and testing practice should be equal in time for maximum benefit.

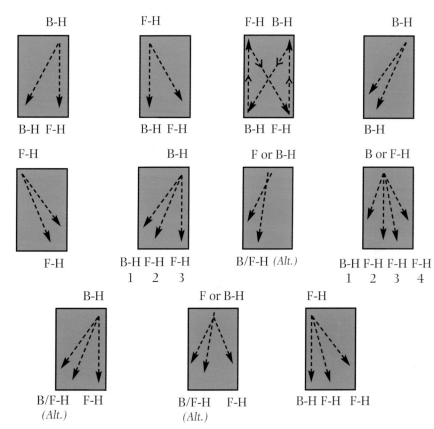

▶ *Fig. 14 Technical practice: testing*
----------- = at random

Tactical development and practice

There are three stages of tactical development:

- keeping the ball in play
- developing accuracy to a large range of targets
- applying pressure with spin, speed and by striking the ball early to different targets.

Coaching tip

Practise consistency, accuracy and applying pressure on your opponent by selecting targets on both the table and your opponent.

▶ *Fig. 15 Tactical practice*
● *Denotes a target on the table where a backhand stroke becomes a forehand.*
X *Denotes the target on your opponent where a backhand stroke becomes a forehand. Against a right-handed player this will be their right hip.*

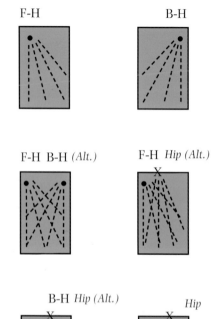

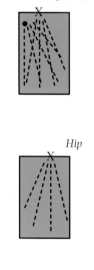

Use of the robot and multi-ball

Practices may include the use of a 'robot'. This is a machine that shoots balls out at pre-set speeds and spins. If used properly, robots are useful aids for improving stroke production (showing practice) and for a single player if he does not have an available partner.

Multi-ball practice is also popular. This is when a coach 'feeds' a number of balls in quick succession to a player. This is better than using a 'robot' because the feeder can vary the spin, speed and positioning of the ball (testing practice) to offer a more realistic practice. This type of practice is physically very demanding.

The ETTA skills award scheme lists more practices that are suitable for players of different standards.

34

Fun games

Table tennis is fun and there are numerous variations of the main game that can be used to maintain the enjoyment while retaining a competitive element.

Overtaking

The players balance the ball on their bats and run around the outside of the playing area. Anyone who is overtaken or who drops the ball is out.

This can be advanced with players bouncing the ball on their bat – either forehand, backhand or alternating forehand and backhand.

Minute rallies

Two players play a rally and count the number of strokes played in one minute.

A variation is to count the number of strokes played without a mistake.

Round the table

All players are at one end of the table with a feeder at the other end. After hitting the ball, each player must run around the table to rejoin the line.

A variation is to have equal numbers at each end of the table and the players run to the opposite end after hitting the ball. Players have three lives, one of which is forfeited on each mistake.

Team singles

One player from each team plays a point. The losing player is replaced by the next member of his team for the second point. A player winning three points in a row must retire.

Targets

● A small target (e.g. a postcard) is placed on the table. Two players play a rally on one diagonal (where the target is) and score points as normal. If they hit the target they score two points.

● A target (e.g. an A3 sheet of paper) is placed on either side of the net. Each player serves alternately, aiming to hit the target. When the target has been hit three times, the paper is folded in half. Each player aims to make his target smaller than his opponent's.

● In teams, players serve to various targets of differing sizes, scoring points if they are successful. Points may be allocated according to difficulty (size, position).

Cricket

Each team has a minimum of three players. One team bats and the other fields. One of the fielding team throws the ball underarm over the net (at head height) to bounce on the opposite side of the table. The batsman hits the ball so that it lands on the opposite side of the table and then on the floor before the fielders can catch him out. If successful he scores a run and continues his innings. He remains in until he misses the ball; he hits the ball into the net; he misses the table; or he is caught out. When all players on the batting side have had an innings, the teams change over.

Relays

In teams, the first player runs to the table and serves the ball. He then runs around the table and catches the ball after it has bounced once and before it hits the floor. If successful, he scores one point and he runs to give the ball to the next player in his team. The first team to score ten points wins. The service should be legal.

A variation is to catch the ball after two bounces or to serve to a specific target.

Programme planning

To be successful at table tennis, it is essential that your training programme is well organised and carefully planned. A single session may be organised as follows:

- warm-up   5 minutes
- knock-up   10 minutes
- showing practice   35 minutes
- testing practice   35 minutes
- conditional play   15 minutes
- match play   15 minutes
- cool-down   5 minutes.

When more than one session is planned, a physical training programme should be incorporated. This should include work on stamina, speed, flexibility and strength.

Physical training is an important part of programme planning. The intensity of the physical training will depend on the age and the standard of the players. Obviously, casual players will not be interested in physical training, but those whose aspirations are higher will understand the need for total fitness.

Physical training can be performed on or off the table. Multi-ball drills are ideal for on-table exercises, as are shadow play exercises.

Most stamina and flexibility work is practised off the table. This includes distance running, skipping and a variety of stretching exercises.

The serious competitor needs to make long-term plans. This is called 'periodisation'. The aim is to train so that the player can 'peak' for important competitions.

A periodised yearly cycle for juniors would include three phases:

- preparation
- competition
- rest.

The preparation phase would be from July to early September. This time is used to concentrate on improving technique and tactical awareness.

In the northern hemisphere the competition phase runs from September to the end of May. This is when players are competing in various competitions and trying to gain the best possible results.

The rest phase is in June when competitions have finished. This is not an inactive time but it is a time when players participate in other sports to maintain their fitness without getting stale by playing too much table tennis.

The timings of these phases will vary depending on the level of play. For example, the European Youth Championships take place in July and this would be included in the competition phase.

Coaching

The ETTA have produced a skills award scheme which has ten different grades. This offers a differentiated programme of practices which are suitable for all levels of players.

Players who wish to improve their playing standards will need to have some coaching. Many schools run table tennis clubs where there is a member of staff who has some expertise. However, for a player to proceed further up the ladder of success, he will need to join a club. Lists of local clubs can be found in libraries or by contacting the National Governing Body.

Once in a club, players will be able to progress through the Coaching Scheme. If they reach national potential, they will be able to attend the National Academy and hopefully play for their country.

English Table Tennis Association skills award scheme

The awards are open to all young players and are suitable for people with disabilities.

The awards are promoted by the English Table Tennis Association Ltd and the English Schools Table Tennis Association.

They have been devised by teachers and coaches to be fun yet challenging. Each award is progressive and easy to administer. Awards may be assessed by teachers, coaches and table tennis organisers.

The purpose of the ETTA skills award scheme is to encourage young players to develop their table tennis skills and so want to play the game at a higher level. Candidates are given every encouragement to succeed. There is no limit to the number of times that a candidate can attempt each test, although there should be a period of practice between each attempt.

There are ten awards; Grades 1 and 2 Polybat are specifically designed for players with disabilities; Grades 1–5 link in with the Youth Sports Trust BT TOP Sport Table Tennis and are introductory awards to whet the appetite for playing table tennis; Grades 1–3 Advanced require correct stroke production and are more challenging for the young player. The tests for each of these awards are detailed on the following pages.

Polybat tests

Grade One Polybat

1. Hit ball over halfway line – forehand x 5
2. Hit ball over halfway line – backhand x 5
3. Serve ball over halfway line – forehand x 5
4. Serve ball over halfway line – backhand x 5
5. Hit ball – forehand x 5
6. Hit ball – backhand x 5
7. Hit moving ball – forehand x 5
8. Hit moving ball – backhand x 5

Class A players achieve 5 tasks
Class B players achieve 6 tasks
Class C players achieve 7 tasks
Class D players achieve 8 tasks

Grade Two Polybat

1. Hit ball using sides – forehand x 5
2. Hit ball using sides – backhand x 5
3. Hit ball to right corner x 5
4. Hit ball to left corner x 5
5. Serve ball to right corner x 5
6. Serve ball to left corner x 5
7. Return of service – forehand x 5
8. Return of service – backhand x 5
9. Forehand rally x 5
10. Backhand rally x 5

Class A players achieve 6 tasks
Class B players achieve 7 tasks
Class C players achieve 8 tasks
Class D players achieve 9 tasks

Assessor notes

These tests should be conducted on tables using specialised Polybat equipment. Assessors should use their discretion when determining the quality of the candidate's playing ability.

...d move –

...nd move –

bac...

3. Jog and ...ll on bat

4. Bounce ball o... t 5 times – forehand

5. Bounce ball on bat 5 times – backhand

6. Drop and hit ball over net 5 times – backhand push

Grade Two

1. Move and bounce ball on bat – forehand
2. Move and bounce ball on bat – backhand
3. Drop and hit ball over net 5 times – forehand drive
4. Hit moving ball over net x 5 – backhand push
5. Backhand push rally x 5
6. Basic service – forehand or backhand x 3

Grade Three

1. Move quickly and bounce ball on bat – forehand
2. Move quickly and bounce ball on bat – backhand
3. Alternate bouncing on bat x 5
4. Hit moving ball over net x 5 – forehand drive
5. Forehand drive rally x 5
6. Legal service x 3

Grade Four

1. Drop and hit ball over net – backhand drive x 5
2. Backhand drive rally x 5
3. Backhand drive and forehand drive rally x 6
4. Forehand drive with movement x 6
5. Forehand drive controlling direction x 6
6. Service – 3 forehand, 3 backhand

Grade Five

1. Backhand drive and forehand drive with movement
2. Backhand drive controlling direction
3. Forehand drive controlling direction
4. Service length – 3 short and 3 long (backhand and forehand)
5. Service direction – 3 line and 3 diagonal (backhand and forehand)
6. Smash x 3

Assessor notes

Candidates should be able to hold bat with the correct grip when performing each of the strokes described.

Grade One Advanced

1. Backhand push rally x 30
2. Forehand drive rally x 30
3. Backhand drive rally x 30
4. Forehand push rally x 15
5. Service x 10
6. Return of service x 10 – short and long, backhand and forehand

Grade Two Advanced

1. Combined forehand and backhand drive V x 30
2. Control of forehand and backhand drive V x 30
3. Combined forehand and backhand push H x 30
4. Combined forehand and backhand push X x 30
5. Service variation x 10
6. Return of varied services x 10

Key to strokes

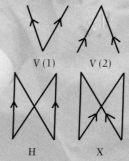

Grade Three Advanced

1. Alternate topspin and backspin x 10 – forehand and backhand
2. Alternate topspin and push x 10 – forehand and backhand
3. Backhand to backhand topspin and then smash x 5
4. Advanced serve (pendulum) x 10
5. Third ball attack x 5
6. Game situation – tactical awareness

Assessor notes

Candidates attempting the advanced tests should show good stroke production and consistency of play.

Further information

Further information and award packs can be obtained by contacting:

The Skills Award Administrator
English Table Tennis Association Ltd
Queensbury House
Havelock Road
Hastings
East Sussex
TN34 1HF

tel: 01424 722525
fax: 01424 422103
email: teachandtrain.etta@talk21.com
website: www@etta.co.uk

Competitive play

The newcomer to table tennis probably began by playing at a school, youth club or local table tennis club. As progress is made, competitive play is necessary. The English Schools Table Tennis Association (ESTTA) runs individual and team competitions for both boys and girls. These are open to any player who attends an affiliated school. The English Table Tennis Association (ETTA) is responsible for co-ordinating a programme of tournaments throughout the country for cadet (under 15 years), junior (under 18 years), senior (over 18 years) and veteran (over 40 years) players. These tournaments include singles and doubles events, and age group and ability banded competitions.

There are also British League competitions for junior, senior and veteran players.

In addition to these 'open' events, there are a large number of 'closed' tournaments. These all have some restrictions. For example a 'Country Closed' is only for players who live in a particular area.

All of these provide valuable match experience and will help a talented player to be noticed by the selectors and perhaps be invited to join county, regional or national squad training camps.

Affiliation

An affiliated player is one who attaches himself to the national association, either directly or through membership of a club or affiliated organisation.

National governing bodies include:

The English Table Tennis Association Ltd (*See* address on page 2.)

The English Schools Table Tennis Association
36 Froom Street
Chorley
Lancashire
PR6 0AN

The Irish Table Tennis Association Ltd
46 Lorcan Villas
Santry
Dublin 9

The Scottish Table Tennis Association
Caledonia House
South Gyle
Edinburgh
EH12 9DQ

The Table Tennis Association of Wales
31 Maes y Celyn
Griffithstown
Pontypool
Gwent
NP4 5DG

The basic principles and techniques used when working with disabled players are the same as those used when coaching and working with able-bodied players.

The major area that coaches need to concentrate on is that of communication.

Deaf and hearing-impaired players

- When talking to players, remember always to face the person you are speaking to.
- Speak normally, even when a person is lip reading.
- Do not shout.
- Demonstrate shots and techniques.
- If necessary, write down information.

Blind and visually-impaired players

- Experiment with the size and colour of the balls used.
- Ensure the playing area is clear of any obstacles.
- Allow players time to orientate themselves in the hall and playing areas.
- Do not move equipment without informing the players.
- Do not walk away from players without telling them.

Learning disability

- Impart information in small pieces.
- Be prepared to go over and repeat instructions/information.
- Be patient.
- Keep checking for understanding.
- Treat the player according to his age.
- Always speak to the player, but if unsure, check with the parent or carer.

Physical impairment

Standing

- No real difference – communication for all physically impaired players is not a problem unless they have a secondary disability.
- Take into account players' mobility and need for use of crutches or sticks.
- If in doubt, ask the player.

Wheelchair users

- Check whether the wheelchair is suitable for physical activity – if the player is able to hold his body erect, coaches may try removing arm rests to allow additional movement. Ask the player first.
- For beginners it is normally appropriate to play with the brakes on, but as they progress they can experiment playing with the brakes off – if the player feels confident.
- When talking to a wheelchair user for any length of time, sit or kneel to make it more comfortable for the player.
- Do not lean on the wheelchair, as this is part of the player's personal space.

These are just some general ideas which should prove useful, but remember: if in doubt always ask the player.

Health and safety

Remember that you are required by law to deliver a greater duty of care when working with disabled people.

If the fire alarm sounds, ensure any deaf or hearing-impaired people are made aware.

If required to evacuate, ensure any blind or visually-impaired players are assisted as appropriate.

If wheelchair users are participating in a session, ensure all gangways and exits are kept sufficiently clear of obstacles.

Ensure that the table tennis table does not have a bar across the end – if it does it should be a minimum of 40 cm (16 in) from the end of the table. If it is less than this amount one option is to cover the bar with foam rubber so that if the wheelchair player does hit it with his legs, there is some protection.

For further information, contact the National Development Officer for People with Disabilities at the ETTA headquarters office or e-mail: judyrogers.etta@talk21.com